6
MINUTE
MORNING
ARMS

6 MINUTE MORNING ARMS

LUCY WYNDHAM-READ

Bath · New York · Singapore · Hong Kong · Cologne · Delhi · Melbourne

First published by Parragon in 2009

Parragon
Queen Street House
4 Queen Street
Bath BA1 1HE, UK

ISBN: 978-1-4075-7229-1

Printed in Malaysia
Created and produced by Ivy Contract
Design: JC Lanaway
Photography: Ian Parsons
Hair and Make-up: Sarah El Hini
Model: Willow Boswell-Wright

The views expressed in this book are those of the author but they are general views
only and readers are urged to consult a relevant and qualified specialist for individual
advice in particular situations. Parragon hereby excludes all liability to the extent
permitted by law for any errors or omissions in this book and for any loss, damage
or expense (whether direct or indirect) suffered by a third party relying on any
information contained in this book.

Ivy Contract would like to thank iStock/Michael Tupy for permission to reproduce
copyright material on pages 6–7.

Thanks to Inter Sport of Lewes in the UK for providing props for photography.

Caution
Please check with your doctor/therapist before attempting this workout,
particularly if you are suffering from an injury, are pregnant or have just had a baby.
It is recommended that new mothers wait at least six weeks post partum before
participating in exercise (12 weeks if it was a Caesarean birth). If you feel any pain or
discomfort at any point, please stop exercising immediately and seek medical advice.

CONTENTS

INTRODUCTION   6

WARMING UP   10

STANDING EXERCISES   16

SEATED EXERCISES   30

FLOOR EXERCISES   36

COOLING DOWN   42

TWO-WEEK PLAN   44

INDEX   48

INTRODUCTION

The arms and upper body is an area that is often overlooked when undertaking exercise routines. This can result in the muscles becoming weak and saggy, which may lead to poor posture and even health problems.

By exercising your arms and upper body you can achieve an incredibly toned and svelte shape. Exercising will also help to naturally lift your bust, banish any wobble from your arms, shape and tone your shoulders, define your back and increase your upper body strength.

Working on your upper body also helps to re-align your muscles, which will enhance your posture and immediately make you look slimmer and more confident.

Clothing
Wear clothes made from a comfortable and breathable fabric which you can remove in layers.

Your arms and upper body contain some major muscle groups, so working on this area will naturally raise your metabolic rate. As well as toning and increasing your strength, you will also be 'melting away' any excess calories by working harder.

The easy-to-follow exercises within this book have been specially designed to target all the areas of the upper body, including the back of the upper arms, the shoulders, the bust and the back. In as little as 6 minutes a day, you can have a beautifully toned upper body and arms that you can show off with confidence instead of hiding under long-sleeved shirts and jumpers!

How to use this book

Simply choose six of the exercises from the book. Always start with the warm up and stretches then finish off with the cool down routines. Try to follow the exercises on a daily basis. There is a wide selection to choose from to keep your training varied and maintain your motivation.

If you look at the two-week plan (see page 44) you will see how to fit the warm up and the exercises into 6 minutes. We've made it easy for you to see what you should be doing on each day.

What you need

Some of the exercises require hand weights. These come in different sizes so you can lift slightly heavier ones as you increase your upper body fitness. We have used 1 kg (purple) and 2 kg (blue) weights. Women can use either weight for any of the exercises, or no weight at all if you prefer. If you don't have any weights, plastic milk jugs filled with either rice grains or sand are a great alternative. It is a good idea to perform your exercises in front of a mirror so you can assess your technique. Always make sure the room is well ventilated and well lit and that you have enough room to stretch your arms fully upwards and out to the side.

It is best to wear layers of breathable, comfortable fabric. It's also worth having a clock visible, with a second hand, so you can time yourself for each exercise. You will need a chair for a couple of the exercises as well as a mat or a towel for the floor exercises.

What time of the day to exercise

If you have enough time, doing these exercises in the morning is a great way to kick start your day as this will speed up your metabolic rate and you will burn off more calories. You will also feel virtuous for the rest of the day knowing you have done your exercises! But the great thing with a 6-minute workout is that you should always be able to find time in the day to squeeze it in.

Getting started

First, use the two-week planner at the back of the book to get started. If you want to develop your own two-week plan later on you can. After warming up, choose six of the 30-second exercises and repeat them so you are working for 6 minutes in total.

The results of toning

Some women get worried that if they do toning exercises for their upper body they will bulk up. This is simply not true – women do not have enough testosterone to build large muscles. You would have to be lifting heavy weights and following a strict strength-training workout!

Equipment
The basic equipment you need to perform the exercises are a mat, weights and a sturdy chair.

This exercise programme is designed to create long, lean, defined muscles rather than muscle bulk. For men using this book it is recommended to use weights with all the arm exercises. The reason for this is that men tend to have a little bit more upper body strength, and it is important for every exercise to feel challenging. By using the hand weights you can be sure that your workout is at the right intensity.

Improving your upper body area

Achieving a super-toned body requires a combination of two forms of exercise: the first is toning, as described in this book, and the other is aerobic. The aerobic form of activity will help to burn off any excess body fat as well as improve your cardiovascular health. You should also not forget the importance of eating sensibly, as too many calories in your diet may increase your level of body fat.

About your muscles

To tone and shape your upper body it is helpful to have a clear understanding of the names and positions of the muscles of the upper body so you know which ones to focus on if you want to tackle any problem areas. It's important to keep the workout balanced by training all the muscles.

Shoulders

The muscles that form your shoulders are known as the deltoids and consist of three sections or heads. Each of these sections has different actions:

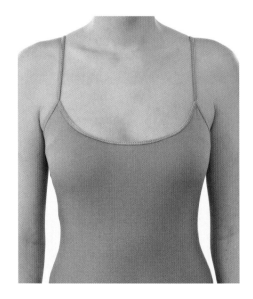

• The anterior (front) originates at the collarbone and moves your arms up and forward, as well as rotating inwards.
• The lateral (side) head works primarily to lift your arms to the side and assist the anterior and posterior heads in their movements.
• The posterior (back) head attaches to your shoulder blade and moves your arms to the rear as well as rotating them outwards.

Chest

The pectoralis major is a large, fan-shaped muscle, which has several attachments. One portion fastens to the middle and inner parts of your collarbone, working with the front of your shoulder to move your arms in front, above and rotate them inwards. The other part attaches to your breastbone and ribs − this muscle is activated by moving your arms only in a downward or forward movement of both arms.

Middle and lower back

The latissimus dorsi is the largest muscle in the upper body and covers the middle and lower back. This muscle is responsible for the downward movements of the upper arm and the inward rotation of your shoulders.

Measure your progress

If you exercise regularly, you will soon see results, so a great way to keep motivated is to measure your progress. There are two ways of doing this.

Firstly, try measuring your arms. Using your right arm, place a tape measure around the upper part of the arm, approximately a hand's distance down from your shoulder. Do this every two weeks, making sure you always measure in the same spot. You should notice the measurement becomes less as the muscle of the upper arms becomes more toned and you reduce excess fat.

Secondly, to see how much you have increased your upper body fitness, try performing a press up using the correct technique (see page 37) and see how many you can comfortably manage. Your performance should quickly improve.

Upper arms

The biceps is the muscle that runs down the front of your upper arm. It allows you to flex your elbow and rotate your forearm so that your palms can face down. This muscle is attached to the shoulder joint and your elbow joint.

The muscle at the back of the upper arm is called the triceps. It is attached to the shoulder and the elbow and it is activated by straightening through the arm. This muscle can easily lose its tone and is often referred to as 'auntie's arms' or 'bingo wings'.

Press ups

Make a note of the number of press ups you do. You should find that press ups become easier the more you do and you can perform more each time.

It is always essential to warm up before undertaking any form of exercise. Without an effective warm up you are likely to injure yourself while working out and you will be unable to perform your exercises efficiently.

WARMING UP

Warming up naturally increases your core body temperature, which then warms up the muscles and makes them more pliable. It also increases the fluid in your joints, which enables you to be more flexible. Even though your toning exercises only take 6 minutes you still need to warm up as injuries can occur at any time.

Marching on the spot

This is a very easy and safe way to gently start warming up your body. Stand with good posture, by having your feet hip-width distance apart, knees soft, stomach pulled in and shoulders pulled back. Starting from this position ensures you are exercising in a safe manner. Begin marching on the spot. Be sure to keep your upper body straight and your stomach muscles pulled in. Aim to gradually lift your knees to hip height and then bend your arms and swing them back and forth as you would do if you were walking fast. Do this for between 2 to 3 minutes until you feel fully warmed up. Alternatively, you can warm up by going for a brisk walk around the block or, if you are in a gym, by using the bike or treadmill.

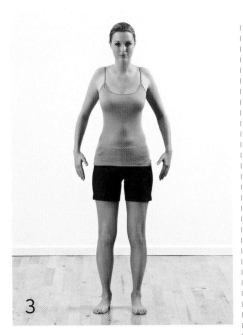

Shoulder Rolls

This will ensure that you have fully warmed through the shoulders and chest and mobilized into the shoulder joint.

1 Stand with good posture and check that your feet are slightly wider than hip-width apart.

2 Make sure your knees are slightly bent and that your abdominal muscles are pulled in tight towards your spine.

3 Very slowly and gently, start to rotate through your shoulders by lifting your shoulders up, then behind. Each time, increase this movement and aim to make the circles bigger.

4 Repeat the exercise 10 times.

Arm Swing

This will increase the flexibility of your chest muscles and help to loosen your upper back.

1 Stand with good posture, knees bent and stomach pulled in.

2 Lift both arms out to either side of your body.

3 In a slow and controlled manner, bring both arms in front so they cross over then back out to either side.

4 Be sure to keep your abdominal muscles pulled in to maintain good posture throughout.

5 Repeat the exercise 10 times.

Stretches

Once you have warmed up, it is also important to stretch your muscles before you start the exercises. You should also do this at the end of your exercises when you cool down.

The benefits of stretching are:

• It reduces the risk of injury during activity.
• It helps prevent post-exercise soreness.
• It improves your flexibility and range of movement.

Deltoid Stretch

1 Stand with good posture, extend one arm out in front of you and cross it in front of the mid-line of your body.

2 Keep both shoulders facing forward. Support the stretching arm on the fleshy part of the forearm.

3 Hold this stretch on each arm for 10 seconds.

WATCH POINT
Breathe normally when practising abdominal hollowing; do not take a deep breath when trying to flatten your stomach. If your ribcage rises during the movement, you have taken a deep breath.

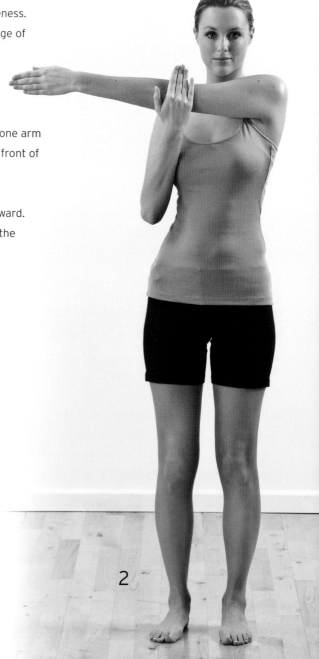

2

Triceps Stretch

1 Stand with good posture, lift one arm above your head and drop the palm of the hand behind the head between the shoulder blades.

2 Lift the other arm and support the stretching arm on the soft, fleshy part of the upper arm or just above the elbow.

3 Hold this stretch on each arm for 10 seconds.

Chest Stretch

If you spend a lot of time using a computer, your shoulders tend to draw in and rise upwards. The chest stretch is good for counteracting this movement and helps to open up the shoulder and chest area.

1 Stand with good posture with your feet slightly apart.

2 Clasp your hands together behind your back, and raise them until your feel the stretch in your chest.

3 Keep your shoulders down as you hold onto your wrists.

4 Hold this position for 10 seconds.

2

Upper Back Stretch

This stretch is particularly good for improving your posture and releasing any tension in your back.

1 Stand with good posture with your feet slightly apart.

2 Keep your knees soft and your stomach pulled in.

3 Take your arms out in front of you and imagine you are hugging a big beach ball. You should feel a stretch across your upper back.

4 Hold this position for 10 seconds.

3

How to Exercise with Good Posture

Good posture is important all the time, but especially when exercising, as you need to be in the correct alignment for the appropriate muscles to be trained to get the best results. Imagine you have a glass sheet in front of you and behind you – this will help keep your body in alignment.

Standing Exercises

1 Stand with your feet just slightly wider than shoulder-width apart.

2 Place your weight evenly through both feet.

3 Extend up through your thighs, squeeze your bottom in and under and pull in your navel to your spine.

4 Stretch up through your spine and let your shoulders drop down from the height of your ears.

5 Contract the abdominal muscles by pulling your navel in towards your spine.

4

4

Seated Exercises

1 Always ensure you use a sturdy chair for the seated exercises.

2 Place your feet hip-width distance apart and make sure your heels are directly under your knees.

3 Sit upright and pull your belly button in towards your spine, as this will protect your back.

4 Pull back your shoulders and keep your chin parallel to the floor.

The following exercises will all be performed standing up. This allows you to have a full range of movement. When lifting weights, always keep the movement slow and controlled. This not only works the muscles harder but it also prevents any injuries.

Triceps Squeeze Back

This is an easy-to-perform standing exercise that will tone through the back of your upper arms creating a long, toned triceps muscle and banishing any wobbly arms. The other great thing with this exercise is that it also stretches your chest muscles, which helps promote good posture.

1 Stand with good posture and your knees slightly bent. Hold the weights keeping your arms by your side, with your palms facing away from you backwards.

2 Lift your chest and pull your shoulders back.

3 Lift both arms directly behind you, and feel this working through your triceps. Hold your arms at the highest point, then slowly lower back to the start position.

WATCH POINT

This is a small lift, so don't expect to raise your arms too high. Keep your knees slightly bent and your abdominal muscles pulled in tight.

1

3

STANDING EXERCISES

WATCH POINT
The arm that supports
your exercising arm
keeps the elbow in line
with your shoulder.

Triceps Pony Tail

This standing triceps exercise is one of
the best ways to tone flabby upper arms.

1 Stand with good posture. Bend your
knees slightly and pull in your stomach.
Place a weight in your right hand, then
extend the right arm straight up and
support it with the other arm. Keep a good
posture and your abdominal muscles
pulled in.

2 Now simply bend at the elbow of
your extended arm so the weight is by
your upper back. Slowly straighten the arm
back up to the start position. Do all your
repetitions on one arm and then repeat
on the other arm.

1

2

To get your abdominal muscles working, make sure you keep your stomach pulled in tight to your spine. Also, be sure not to arch your back.

Bell Pull

This exercise works on toning your arms through your biceps and triceps as well as toning your chest muscle. This is great for women as it helps lift and tone the bust as well as giving the arms a fabulous workout.

1 Stand with good posture, knees slightly bent and your feet hip-width apart.

2 Lift your arms to shoulder height and then bend at the elbows, so your arms form an L-shape. Press your arms together and keep elbows at shoulder height.

3 Take a deep breath in and then, as you breathe out, gently lift your arms a little bit higher, hold for a second, then lower slowly again. Do all your repetitions on one arm and then repeat on the other arm.

3

2

Standing Wall Press Up

This exercise is a fantastic way to build upper body strength as well as tone through the back of your upper arm muscles and into your chest.

1 Stand at arms' length away from a wall, with your feet shoulder-width apart. Place your hands against the wall, with your arms stretched out in front of you and your fingers pointing to the ceiling.

2 Keeping your back straight and your head looking straight in front of you, slowly bend your arms at the elbows.

3 Aim to lower yourself a little way towards the wall and then push back to your start position.

WATCH POINT

If you want to increase the level of difficulty, try moving your legs further back. Also, keeping your abdominal muscles pulled in will help tone your stomach muscles.

WATCH POINT

Keep your elbows slightly bent while performing this to avoid locking out your elbow joints.

2

Shoulder Press

This will help to tone through your shoulders and triceps as well as promote good upper body posture.

1 Stand with good posture, knees slightly bent and stomach pulled in. Hold a weight in each hand at shoulder height.

2 With your palms facing forwards and keeping your head level, press the weights overhead, extending your elbows.

3 Bring the weights together as you press them, hold for a second then slowly lower to the start position.

1

3

2

3

Upright Pull

This exercise focuses on toning through your shoulders, biceps and back, which will help you achieve a beautifully toned upper body.

1 Stand with your feet shoulder-width apart and your knees slightly bent.

2 Hold a weight in each hand, side by side at thigh level, keeping your palms facing towards your thighs.

3 Slowly bring the weights up towards your collarbone, until your elbows are about shoulder height. Keep your shoulders down and relaxed as you lift. If you find you are shrugging your shoulders up towards your ears, your weights may be too heavy.

4 Slowly lower the weights to the start position.

WATCH POINT
Ensure you keep your weights close to your body as you lift and lower them.

3 Slowly lift the weights out to the sides to shoulder level, keeping your elbows slightly bent. Keep your shoulders down and relaxed as you lift. If you find you are shrugging your shoulders up towards your ears, your weights may be too heavy.

4 Slowly lower the weights back to your start position.

WATCH POINT

It's important to keep a slight bend in both arms as you lift them. Imagine both arms are pouring water from a kettle, as this helps to keep the arms soft.

Side Shoulder Raise

This exercise will help to define your shoulders – it is also good for improving flexibility throughout your shoulder joints and will give you good posture.

1 Stand with your feet shoulder-width apart and your knees slightly bent.

2 Hold the hand weights at your sides at thigh level.

3

4

Turning Press

This is a great time-saving exercise, as it targets several upper body muscles at once, including your triceps, biceps and shoulders.

1 Stand with your feet hip-width apart, upper body straight, knees soft and stomach pulled in.

2 Hold a weight in each hand with the palms facing directly in front of your shoulders and your elbows bent as if in a biceps curl (see page 35).

3 Straighten elbows and lift weights overhead, twisting the hands until the palms face out. Lower your arms and twist your palms to face in again.

Front Raises

This exercise will sculpt your shoulders and create tone and definition through the front of your arms.

1 Stand with good posture, your feet hip-width apart and knees soft.

2 Keep your abdominal muscles tight and chest relaxed.

3 Hold a weight in each hand with palms facing in, weights by your thighs.

4 In a slow and controlled smooth move, lift both arms up forwards and straight to shoulder height, then slowly lower both arms back to the start position.

STANDING EXERCISES

1

2

Standing Long Arm Palm Press

This exercise strengthens the front
and the middle of your shoulders.

1 Holding a weight in each hand, stand
with good upright posture, knees soft,
stomach pulled in and with your feet
shoulder-width apart.

2 Lift both arms up and out to your
sides so your wrists are in line with
your shoulders, and have your palms
facing upwards.

3 Now lift both arms up above your head,
keeping the arms long. Try to bring
your hands together to touch and hold for
a second. Now very slowly lower your arms
back to the start position.

3

WATCH POINT
When your arms are
out to your sides, keep
them parallel to your
shoulders, not any
higher or lower.

Front Arm Toner (Hammer Curl)

This tones through the front of your upper arms and also works on strengthening your forearm muscles.

1 Stand with your feet shoulder-width apart, knees soft, elbows fixed and stomach pulled in tight to promote good upper body posture.

2 With a weight in each hand, let both arms hang down long by the side of your body, fully straightened with your palms facing in towards your body.

3 Simultaneously lift your weights upwards, without moving your elbows, hold for a second then slowly lower back to your start position.

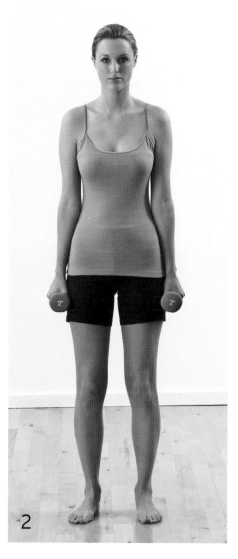

Arm Opener

This exercise works by toning the biceps in your front upper arms. The exercise will firm the biceps, not bulk them out.

1 Stand with your feet shoulder-width apart, knees soft, elbows fixed and stomach pulled in tight to promote good upper body posture.

2 Have your arms by your side with your elbows bent and your arms in an L-shape, a weight in each hand.

3 With your palms facing in towards each other, slowly open your forearms out to either side, whilst still keeping your elbows tucked into your sides. Hold for a second then slowly return to a start position.

WATCH POINT
Keep this exercise slow and controlled. It is important to keep your elbows locked in tight to your side.

Arm Circles

This easy-to-follow exercise will improve mobility and definition in your shoulders. You can increase the intensity by using hand weights or by simply creating bigger circles.

1 Stand straight with your feet shoulder-width apart. Your arms should be straight out to the sides so that your body forms a T-shape.

2 Starting slowly, make small, circular motions with both arms, clockwise.

3 Focus on keeping your knees soft and your abdominal muscles pulled in throughout.

WATCH POINT
The stronger you feel, the bigger you can make the circles.

3

Chest Press

This exercise targets two muscles – your triceps and your chest muscle. This is a great exercise for women, as it tightens the muscles that support your bust, giving you a good bust lift.

1 Stand with good upright posture, knees soft and your feet hip-width apart.

2 Using a weight in each hand, bend your arms so your hands are in front of your shoulders.

3 Gently extend your arms straight out, keeping them at shoulder height.

4 Hold for a second when your arms are fully extended. Slowly return your arms to the start position.

WATCH POINT

Focus on engaging your abdominal muscles, by pulling your navel tight to your spine. This helps protect your back.

2

3

Arm Shaper (Boxing Arms)

This is a really fun exercise that will tone your arms, chest and shoulders. When an exercise works several muscles at once it increases the amount of calories you burn, both during and after the exercise.

1 Stand up straight with your feet shoulder-width apart, stomach pulled in and your knees slightly bent.

2 Hold your hands level against your upper chest with both your fists clenched and palms facing inwards.

3 Punch one arm forward under control, with your knuckles facing forwards. Make sure your hands are level and kept at shoulder height.

4 Bring your hand back to start position, slowly and under control, and then punch forwards with the opposite arm.

WATCH POINT
Keep your knees soft and your stomach pulled in. This will not only work your stomach muscles but will also protect your back.

STANDING EXERCISES

Bust Lift

This exercise targets the chest muscle, which is responsible for supporting the bust. If this muscle is not exercised it will become less supportive, which means the bust begins to droop. This is a great way of toning and giving yourself a bust lift.

1 Stand upright with good posture, knees slightly bent, feet hip-width distance apart and stomach pulled in.

2 Extend your arms out in front of you at chest height, bend the elbows and join the hands by the palms facing into each other.

3 Stay in this position, press into your palms and, holding this squeeze, slowly lift your palms a little bit higher. Hold for a second while still applying the squeeze then slowly lower to the start position, release the squeeze for a second then re-apply and lift.

WATCH POINT
Keep this very slow and controlled. The more pressure you apply through the squeeze the harder you work on lifting the bust.

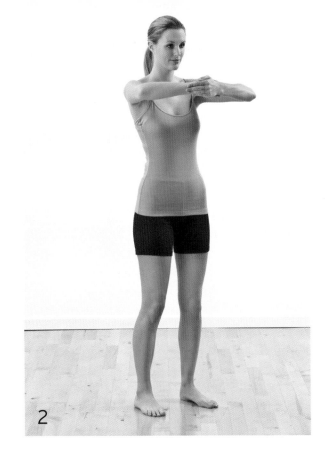

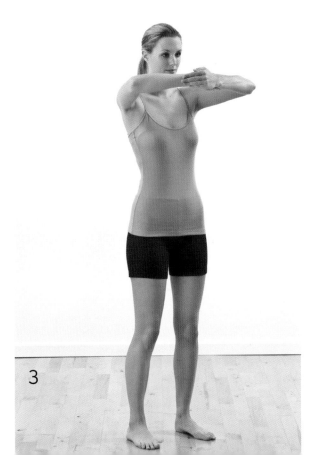

SEATED EXERCISES

For the following seated exercises always ensure you use a sturdy chair. These exercises will again target all the muscles through your upper body helping to tone and define.

Triceps Kick Back

This exercise isolates the back of the upper arm, specifically targeting the troublesome area sometimes referred to as 'auntie's arms' or 'bingo wings'.

1 Kneel over a chair, with one arm supporting your body and one knee bent on the chair. Ensure that the elbow of the supporting arm stays soft and that the knee of the leg extended to the floor is also soft.

2 With your weight in one hand, position your upper arm so it is parallel to the floor and bent at the elbow.

3 Slowly extend the arm until it is straight, then slowly return and repeat. Do all your repetitions on one arm and then repeat on the other arm, by turning around and placing your opposite leg on the chair.

WATCH POINT
For a greater range of motion, the upper arm can be positioned with the elbow at a slightly higher angle than the shoulder.

2

3

Triceps Dips

This exercise specifically works on toning your triceps by working both arms in one move. You will notice how quickly this muscle tones up and that this exercise will feel easier each week as the arms become fitter.

1 Sit right on the edge of your chair, with your hands next to your hips and your palms face down.

2 Place your feet firmly on the floor hip-width apart and with your knees bent.

3 Lift up onto your hands and bring your hips slightly forwards.

4 Bend your elbows and lower your hips down, keeping them very close to the chair. Keep your abdominal muscles pulled in and shoulders down.

5 In a controlled manner, slowly push back up without locking the elbows.

WATCH POINT
Make sure you keep your hips close to the chair, to keep the focus on your triceps and not on your shoulders.

3

4

Extended triceps dips
To make this exercise harder, simply walk your feet out a little way. Equally, to make it easier, move your feet closer in.

Bent-Over Arm Shaper

This seated exercise will target your arms and your upper back muscles and improve your upper body flexibility and posture.

1 Using a weight in each hand, sit on the edge of your chair, bent over, with arms hanging down, feet slightly apart.

2 Keep your abdominal muscles pulled in to stop you collapsing your back onto your legs.

3 Lift your arms out to the sides, up to shoulder level, squeezing your shoulder blades together.

4 Keep the elbows slightly bent and only lift to your shoulders. Lower the arms and repeat.

WATCH POINT

To make sure you keep your arms slightly bent, imagine you are pouring water from a kettle.

1

3

Seated Back Toner

This trains the upper part of your arms, through your deltoid muscle.

1 Sit with good posture, feet hip-width apart and stomach pulled in.

2 Holding a weight in each hand, lift your elbows up to shoulder height, then bend them so that your wrists are by your chest and your elbows are in line with your shoulders.

3 Using your weights, slowly squeeze both elbows behind you, maintaining the bend and keeping your elbows parallel to the floor. Hold for a second then slowly return to the start position.

WATCH POINT
Aim to squeeze your shoulder blades together as you move your arms behind you.

Criss-cross Arms

This simple exercise tones your triceps, biceps and chest muscles.

1 Sit with good posture, arms extended out in front of you, palms facing each other.

2 Cross your right arm over the left, turning your palms down along the way. Pause, then return to the starting position.

3 Do all your repetitions on one arm and repeat on the other arm.

WATCH POINT
Focus on keeping your abdominal muscles pulled in throughout. To make this more of a challenge, try using weights.

2

WATCH POINT
Try to focus on just bending through the elbows and aim to keep the shoulder joint very still.

Arms Out Biceps Curl

This exercise tones your biceps as well as engages your triceps, as this muscle has to stabilize the arms in the exercise position.

1 Sit on your chair with good upright body posture, knees bent and feet firmly on the floor, slightly apart.

2 Using a weight in each hand, lift both arms, fully extended, out to your sides, to shoulder height. Turn your palms so they face upwards.

3 Keeping your stomach muscles pulled in, slowly bend your elbows. Aim for your hands to reach your shoulders, hold, then slowly straighten your arms back out.

3

Biceps Curl

This exercise focuses on working the biceps muscle through a full range of motion.

1 Sit leaning forwards with your legs slightly spread and your left hand on your left thigh.

2 Hold a weight in your right hand and at arm's length, your elbow resting against the inside of your knee.

3 From this position, slowly lift your arm upwards to make an L-shape.

4 With the weight at knee height, slowly lift your arm up towards your chest. Hold for a second then lower, then slowly go all the way back to the start position. Repeat on the other arm.

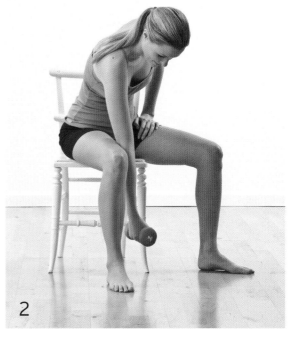

FLOOR EXERCISES

For the following floor exercises it is essential that you use a mat or a towel to exercise on. This is to protect your knees and back. As with the standing and seated exercises, they should all be performed in a slow and controlled manner.

Triceps Bend

This is a fantastic exercise for creating tone and definition through your back arms, as it isolates the triceps muscle that is found at the back of the upper arms. This muscle is toned by extending your arms straight from a bent position.

1 Lie face up on the mat with your knees bent. Hold a weight in each hand.

2 Extend the arms straight up over your chest, palms facing in towards each other, ensuring you have a firm grip of the weights.

3 Slowly bend your elbows and lower your hands down to a few inches above your forehead, to form a 90-degree angle.

4 Squeeze the triceps muscle by slowly straightening your arms without locking out your joints.

Kneeling Boxed Press Up

This exercise targets lots of your upper body and arm muscles so it is great for toning your arms, your bust and also for building upper body strength. You will notice the fitter and the more toned your arms become, the stronger you will be, and you should soon be able to perform these with ease.

1 Kneel on the mat with knees directly under your hips. Hands should be slightly wider than shoulder-width apart, with fingers pointing forwards.

2 Keep your body weight over your hands, stomach pulled in tight and your back flat. Slowly lower your body so your elbows are at a 90-degree angle.

3 Gently push yourself back up to the start position.

WATCH POINT
Keep your stomach muscles pulled in to support your back and, if not using a mat, use a towel to protect your knees on the floor.

Boxed press up (advanced)
As you become fitter, make this exercise a little more challenging by pushing your hips forwards from your knees through to your spine, so that your body is in a straight line. This means you are now lifting more of your own body weight.

Superwoman Arms

This will tone through your shoulder and biceps, whilst working to improve your shoulder joint flexibility.

1 Kneel on the mat on all fours, with your wrists directly under your shoulders and your knees under your hips on the mat. Keep your abdominal muscles contracted. Holding a small weight, lift up one arm so that it is in line with your shoulder.

2 Now slowly bend the arm back so your elbow is then in line with your shoulder. Hold, then gently release back to a straight arm and repeat. Do all your repetitions on one arm and then repeat on the other arm.

Back Extensions

It is important for great upper body posture to have strong back muscles. This will help keep you strong and upright whilst also toning through your upper arms.

1 Lie face down the mat and place your fingertips by the side of your head.

2 Contract your abdominal muscles and keep them contracted throughout the exercise.

3 Squeeze the back to lift the chest a little way off the floor. Hold for a second. Then slowly lower back down.

Floor Arm Lift

This is a challenging exercise but it is fantastic for sculpting your upper arms as it really works your triceps.

1 Sit on the mat with your legs straight and together. Place your hands, fingertips forwards, just behind your hips, and point your toes.

2 Pull in your abdominal muscles, straighten your arms (hands should be under your shoulders) and lift your hips off the floor until your body is aligned from shoulders to toes. Keep looking forwards.

3 Hold the position for a second then slowly lower.

WATCH POINT
To make this exercise easier, try doing it with your legs bent.

1

2

Open Flyer

This floor exercise will tone through your chest, shoulders and arms while working on your upper body strength and flexibility.

1 Lie on the mat. Hold a weight in each hand over your chest with your arms up and your palms facing each other.

2 Keeping your elbows slightly bent, lower your arms out to the sides and down until they're level with your chest.

3 Keep your elbows in a fixed position and avoid lowering the weights too low.

4 Squeeze your chest to bring your arms back up, as though you're hugging a tree.

WATCH POINT
The slower you perform this exercise, the more effective it is.

FLOOR EXERCISES

Super Chest Toner

This is a great exercise to work deep into the chest muscles, which can help to support and lift the bust muscle, as well as increase your range of flexibility through your shoulders.

1 Lie on the mat, face up, with your knees bent and feet firmly on the floor.

2 Using a weight in each hand, bend your arms out to the side so they rest on the floor, elbows in line with your shoulders and bent, to form an L-shape.

3 Slowly lift your arms off the floor while maintaining the bend and aim to bring both arms to meet directly in line with your face. Hold for a couple of seconds then slowly lower back to the floor and repeat.

WATCH POINT
By keeping your navel pulled down tight to your spine, you will protect your back throughout this workout. Doing this will also tone your deepest abdominal muscles.

COOLING DOWN

Many people dismiss cooling down after exercise as a waste of time or simply unimportant. In reality, the cool down is just as important as the warm up if you want to stay injury free. However, while the main purpose of warming up is to prepare the body and mind for exercising, cooling down plays a different role.

The main aim of the cool down is to promote recovery and return the body to a pre-exercise level and, if performed properly, to assist your body in its necessary repair process.

The cool down will also help with 'post-exercise muscle soreness'. It does this by allowing the muscles to repair and align themselves after the exercises. This prevents the soreness that is usually experienced the day after a workout, particularly if you haven't done any exercise for a while or if you are a beginner to exercise.

Cooling down and stretching also increases your flexibility, which means you will be able to have a fuller range of movement through your joints.

How to cool down

Before you begin your stretches, it is a good idea to march on the spot for a couple of minutes to gently bring your heart rate and body temperature back to their pre-exercise state. Do this by gradually easing your march to a slow pace and then coming to a halt. Sit on the floor in preparation for the cool-down stretches.

Post-exercise Triceps Stretch

1 Sit comfortably on the mat, cross-legged and with good posture. Lift one arm above your head and drop the palm of the hand behind the head, between the shoulder blades.

2 Lift the other arm and support the stretching arm on the soft, fleshy part of the upper arm or above the elbow.

3 Hold this stretch for 15 seconds. Repeat on the other arm.

2

Post-exercise Deltoid Stretch

1 Sit comfortably on the mat, cross-legged and with good posture. Extend one arm out in front of you and cross it, still fully extended, in front of the mid-line of your body.

2 Keep both shoulders facing forward. Support the stretching arm on the fleshy part of the forearm.

3 Hold this stretch for 15 seconds. Repeat on the other arm.

2

2

Post-exercise Chest Stretch

1 Sit comfortably on the mat, cross-legged and with good posture. Lift your arms out to the sides and place them behind you.

2 Keep the shoulders down as you clasp your hands together.

3 Hold this stretch for 20 seconds.

Post-exercise Upper Back Stretch

1 Sit comfortably on the mat, cross-legged and with good posture. Lift up your arms in front of you.

2 Clasp your hands in front of you and imagine you are hugging a large ball. Feel the stretch in your back.

3 Hold this stretch for 20 seconds.

2

TWO-WEEK PLAN

Here's an easy-to-follow two-week plan. Although the plan suggests that you do a 6-minute routine each day, you can build up the amount of time you spend and the types of exercise you do. You can also pick and mix the routines you choose. You may feel that as you become fitter and stronger that you can increase the number of exercises and minutes you do to a full routine. You will improve tone, flexibility and strength.

How to do the routines

Each daily plan has been designed to give a full workout to all the upper body muscles. Aim to complete the number of repetitions recommended, but don't worry if you can't at first. Soon you will notice your strength and fitness improve. The routines are designed to take 6 minutes, which includes time for you to get into position and have a short rest between each exercise.

Make the most of your workout

- Warm up properly.
- Drink plenty of water to keep fully hydrated.
- Focus on keeping your abdominal muscles pulled in while exercising.
- Keep movements slow and controlled.
- When standing, keep your knees soft.
- Warm up and stretch before your exercises.
- Cool down and stretch properly afterwards.

Day 1

Bell pull: *10-12 reps* **p18**
Side shoulder raise: *10-12 reps* **p21**
Shoulder press: *10-12 reps* **p19**
Standing wall press up: *10-12 reps* **p19**
Triceps squeeze back: *15 reps* **p16**

Day 2

Triceps pony tail: *10 reps on each arm* **p17**
Front arm toner: *10-12 reps* **p24**
Bust lift: *20 reps* **p29**
Upright pull: *10-12 reps* **p20**
Bent-over arm shaper: *10-12 reps* **p32**
Open flyer: *10-12 reps* **p40**

Day 3

Triceps dips: *10–12 reps* **p31**

Biceps curl: *10 reps on each arm* **p35**

Chest press: *10–12 reps* **p27**

Front raises: *10–12 reps* **p22**

Side shoulder raise: *10–12 reps* **p21**

Arm shaper: *10 reps on each arm* **p28**

Back extensions: *10–12 reps* **p38**

Day 5

Front arm toner: *10–12 reps* **p24**

Triceps pony tail: *10 reps on each arm* **p17**

Chest press: *10–12 reps* **p27**

Superwoman arms: *10–12 reps on each arm* **p38**

Triceps dips: *10–12 reps* **p31**

Day 4

Open flyer: *10–12 reps* **p40**

Arms out biceps curl: *10–12 reps* **p34**

Triceps squeeze back: *15 reps* **p16**

Upright pull: *10–12 reps* **p20**

Shoulder press: *10–12 reps* **p19**

Seated back toner: *10–12 reps* **p33**

Day 6

Triceps bend: *10–12 reps* **p36**

Arms out biceps curl: *10–12 reps* **p34**

Bust lift: *20 reps* **p29**

Standing long arm palm press: *10–12 reps* **p23**

Kneeling boxed press up: *10–12 reps* **p37**

Back extensions: *10–12 reps* **p38**

TWO-WEEK PLAN

Day 7

Triceps pony tail: *10 reps on each arm* **p17**

Floor arm lift: *6-8 reps* **p39**

Criss-cross arms: *20 reps on each arm* **p33**

Upright pull: *10-12 reps* **p20**

Seated back toner: *10-12 reps* **p33**

Open flyer: *10-12 reps* **p40**

Day 9

Superwoman arms: *10 reps on each arm* **p38**

Bent-over arm shaper: *10-12 reps* **p32**

Arm opener: *10-12 reps* **p25**

Floor arm lift: *6-8 reps* **p39**

Super chest toner: *10-12 reps* **p41**

Day 8

Arm shaper: *10-12 reps on each arm* **p28**

Side shoulder raise: *10-12 reps* **p21**

Bell pull: *10-12 reps* **p18**

Bust lift: *20 reps* **p29**

Kneeling boxed press up: *8-10 reps* **p37**

Day 10

Bust lift: *20 reps* **p29**

Arm circles: *20 reps* **p26**

Arms out biceps curl: *10-12 reps* **p34**

Boxed press up (advanced): *8-10 reps* **p37**

Superwoman arms: *10 reps on each arm* **p38**

Day 11

Bent-over arm shaper:
10-12 reps **p32**

Triceps kick back: *10 reps
on each arm* **p30**

Criss-cross arms: *20 reps
on each arm* **p33**

Open flyer: *10-12 reps* **p40**

Turning press: *10-12 reps* **p22**

Day 13

Super chest toner: *10-12 reps* **p41**

Arm circles: *20 reps* **p26**

Arm opener: *10-12 reps* **p25**

Back extensions: *10-12 reps* **p38**

Shoulder press: *10-12 reps* **p19**

Day 12

Triceps squeeze back:
15 reps **p16**

Arms out biceps curl:
10-12 reps **p34**

Seated back toner:
10-12 reps **p33**

Chest press: *10-12 reps* **p27**

Arm shaper: *10-12 reps on
each arm* **p28**

Day 14

Extended triceps dips: *10-12 reps* **p31**

Bust lift: *20 reps* **p29**

Front arm toner: *12 reps on each arm* **p24**

Seated back toner: *10-12 reps* **p33**

Super chest toner: *10-12 reps* **p41**

INDEX

arm circles 26

arm opener 25

arm shaper 28

arm swing 11

arms out biceps curl 34

back extensions 38

bell pull 18

bent-over arm shaper 32

biceps curl 35

boxing arms 28

bust lift 29

chest press 27

chest stretches 14, 43

cooling down 42-3

criss-cross arms 33

deltoid stretches 12, 43

equipment 7

floor arm lift 39

floor exercises 36-41

front arm toner 24

front raises 22

hammer curl 24

kneeling boxed press up 37

marching on the spot 10

measuring progress 9

muscles 8-9

open flyer 40

posture for exercises 15

press ups 37

seated back toner 33

seated exercises 30-5

shoulder press 19

shoulder rolls 11

side shoulder raise 21

standing exercises 16-29

standing long arm palm press 23

standing wall press up 19

stretches 12-14, 42-3

super chest toner 41

superwoman arms 38

time to exercise 7

triceps bend 36

triceps dips 31

triceps kick back 30

triceps pony tail 17

triceps squeeze back 16

triceps stretches 13, 42

turning press 22

two-week plan 44-7

upper back stretches 14, 43

upright pull 20

warming up 10-15

weights 7